Bite-Size Pieces
of my Past

A simple fill-in-the-blank workbook, conversation starter, collection of memories, and keepsake.

By Andrea Bargsley Vincent

 www.trafford.com

North America & international
toll-free: 1 888 232 4444 (USA & Canada)
fax: 812 355 4082

ACKNOWLEDGEMENTS

This workbook is dedicated to my grandmother, Verna Dornbluth, whose brilliant mind was taken from her by Alzheimer's Disease before she died in 1987.

My Inspiration

While rifling through a trunk of old keepsakes, I stumbled across this old photo of my father. Prior to finding this photo, I had heard little about my father's relationship with my grandfather. This one photo sparked hours of conversation about the happenings surrounding why it was taken, memories connected to this period of time, and anecdotes about my grandfather's personality.

It is amazing, the emotions and memories conjured by pictures from one's past. Events, places, people, and things that have not come to mind for many years suddenly come alive when we find something special from our past.

This one picture, this one conversation with my father who typically keeps all things emotional to himself, inspired me to put together this special workbook so that anyone can make notes about pieces of their past.

I hope this workbook facilitates meaningful interaction between families, caregivers, and friends. My goal is for everyone to see "seniors" as the individuals they have always been.

Andrea Bargsley Vincent

Introduction

Bite-Size Pieces

The premise of this workbook is to help you determine which piece or pieces of your past you would like to preserve on paper.

The most important gift we can give someone who is nearing their final stage in lie is human interaction.

The Basics

All About You

MY PERSONAL INFORMATION

My name is (including maiden name)

_____

.

I was born in (year) _____ in the town and State of

_____.

The place I lived longest was _____.

My spouse's name is _____.

We were married in the year _____ in the State of

_____ and remained married for

_____ years.

I lived in the following places: _____

_____

_____

I attended _____ elementary school,

_____ junior high, and _____

_____ high school.

The Basics

All About You

MY PERSONAL INFORMATION

I attended the following Universities/Colleges:

_____

_____

_____

where I studied _____

_____ .

I received my degree(s) in _____

_____ .

The clubs and organizations to which I belonged were:

_____

_____ .

My hobbies include:

_____

_____ .

I attend _____ place

of worship.

All About You

MY FAMILY

My mother's full name is _____.

My father's full name is _____:

My ethnic background is _____

_____.

My ancestors came to this country in (year) _____

from (place) _____.

The circumstances surrounding our immigration to

this country were: _____

_____

_____

_____.

The Basics

All About You

MORE ABOUT MY PARENTS

Interesting facts about my parents include: _____

_____

_____

_____

_____ .

The story my mother/father told repeatedly about their

trials and tribulations or childhood was:

_____

_____

_____

_____

_____ .

Some of the controversies my parents faced include:

_____

_____

_____ .

The Basics

Family & Friends

MY FAMILY

I have _____ siblings. Their names and birth years are:

Name _____

Name _____

Name _____

Name _____

I have _____ children. Their names and ages are:

Name _____

Name _____

Name _____

Name _____

My grandchildren's names are:

_____

_____

My great-grandchildren's names are:

_____

_____

The Basics

Family & Friends

Use this page for more information about family.

Family Heritage

Family Heritage

My family on my mother's side comes from

_____.

My family on my father's side comes from

_____.

My mother's family moved to _____

for (what reason) _____

_____

_____.

My father's family moved to _____

for (what reason) _____

_____

_____.

The Basics

More About Me

More Details About Me

Places I've lived include: _____

_____

_____

_____

_____

_____ .

Places I've traveled include: _____

_____

_____

_____

_____

_____

_____ .

The languages I speak include: _____

_____ .

My military service background is: _____

_____

_____ .

Friendly Faces

Memory Triggers are merely questions that help bring people, places, and things from your past back into focus.

FRIENDS & ACQUAINTANCES

The most important people in my life are/were:

_____

_____

_____

_____

_____ .

My best friend is/was:

_____ .

Other people who come to mind include:

_____

_____

_____

_____ .

Memory Triggers

Friendly Faces

Use this page to capture memories about the people just listed on the previous page.

Friendly Faces

My favorite pets of all times:

_____

_____.

My childhood friends:

_____

_____

_____.

My newest friend is:

_____

_____.

The people I would like to thank for shaping my life are:

_____

_____

_____

_____.

Friendly Faces

My mentor was: _____

_____.

Acquaintances with interesting characteristics:

The craziest _____

The wisest _____

The nosey neighbors _____

The saintliest _____

The most intellectual _____

The strangest _____

The meanest _____

The best boss _____

The most talented _____

The best cook _____

The worst cook _____

The most trustworthy _____

Friendly Faces

My immediate family and their distinguishing characteristics:

Aunt(s) _____

_____

_____

Uncle(s) _____

_____

_____

Brother(s) _____

_____

_____

Sister(s) _____

_____

_____

Cousin(s) _____

_____

_____

Memory Triggers

Memory Triggers

Friendly Faces

Use this space for additional details about people you have known and specific details you remember about them.

Memory Triggers

Remembering the Past

This is extra space to write about travels, adventures, and strangers along the way.

Memory Triggers

Remembering the Past

EVENTS AND FEELINGS FROM THE PAST

As a child I always admired: _____
_____.

When I was a teenager, the worst trouble I got into was:
_____
_____.

The worst accident I ever had was: _____
_____
_____.

My fondest memories include:

A trip to _____
_____.

Spending time with mom while doing _____
_____

Summers with _____
_____.

Letters back and forth with _____.

Memory Triggers

Remembering the Past

EVENTS AND FEELINGS FROM THE PAST

Winning the _____

Meeting _____

Collecting _____

Watching _____

Playing with _____

Learning to _____

Visiting with _____

Spending time at _____

Memory Triggers

Remembering the Past

Do you remember a funny story, embarrassing moment, or special occasion that you would like to share? Use this space for any other memorable moments.

Memory Triggers

Remembering the Past

My favorite holiday is _____.

Some of our traditions surrounding this holiday included:

_____

_____

_____.

The first time I felt truly scared was _____

_____

_____.

My first job was _____

_____

_____.

I still get sad when I think about _____

_____

_____

_____.

Remembering the Past

Memory Triggers

My all-time favorite sports team is _____
_____
_____.

Sports that I played include:

☐ football   ☐ baseball   ☐ softball
☐ soccer   ☐ basketball   ☐ tennis
☐ hockey   ☐ track/field   ☐ croquet
☐ swimming   ☐ badminton   ☐ volleyball
☐ other _____

More of my favorite sports teams: _____
_____
_____
_____.

Memory Triggers

Remembering the Past

Meaningful "firsts" in my life:

Friend _____

Job _____

Kiss _____

Debt _____

Childbirth _____

House _____

Car _____

Memory _____

Haircut _____

War _____

National Tragedy _____

Memory Triggers

Remembering the Past

Meaningful "firsts" in my life:

Hero _____

Disappointment _____

Broken Limb _____

Fight _____

Award / Recognition _____

I was the first in my family to _____

_____.

The first thing I learned to cook was _____

_____.

Other firsts in my life: _____

_____

_____

_____

_____

_____.

Memory Triggers

Remembering the Past

Wars in which I participated include: ☐ WWI ☐ WWII
  ☐ Korean ☐ Vietnam

Details I remember about these wars are: _____

_____

_____

_____

_____.

One thing I have taught my grandchildren is: _____

_____.

One tragedy I will never forget is: _____

_____

_____

_____.

Things that make me happy are: _____

_____

_____

_____.

Memory Triggers

Remembering the Past

The happiest day of my life was _____

_____

_____

_____.

I want to be remembered as _____

_____

_____

_____.

Experiences that made me a stronger person include:

_____

_____

_____

_____

_____

_____.

Then vs. Now

How Things Have Changed

Describe how the following things have changed over the past several decades during your lifetime:

Household responsibilities

THEN _____

NOW _____

Communications

THEN _____

NOW _____

Transportation

THEN _____

NOW _____

Technology

THEN _____

NOW _____

Then vs. Now

How Things Have Changed

Family values

THEN _____

NOW _____

Respect

THEN _____

NOW _____

Priorities

THEN _____

NOW _____

Work Ethic

THEN _____

NOW _____

How Things Have Changed

Then vs. Now

Holidays

THEN _____

NOW _____

Education

THEN _____

NOW _____

Political Elections

THEN _____

NOW _____

Health and Lifestyles

THEN _____

NOW _____

How Things Have Changed

Then vs. Now

Are there other things in your life that have changed drastically? How about things that you wish had stayed the same?

Then vs. Now

How Things Have Changed

List a memorable event from each decade of your life:

1920's

1930's

1940's

1950's

1960's

1970's

1980's

1990's

2000's

The Person I am Today

Myself, My Soul

Old ideals that have now taken a back seat:

_____

_____

_____.

My personal sense of style and taste these days:

_____

_____

_____.

Hidden talents I wish I had discovered earlier in life:

_____

_____

_____.

Things I am looking forward to experiencing in the future:

_____

_____

_____.

The Person I am Today

Myself, My Soul

The career I would choose today:

_____

_____

_____ .

One simple way that I have left an impact on my community:

_____

_____

_____ .

The dream I never had a chance to realize:

_____

_____

_____ .

A few things I am glad I will never have to do again:

_____

_____

_____ .

The Person I am Today

Myself, My Soul

Share your wisdom with future generations. What details would you have changed about your life? Is there advice that you can give to those half your age?

Tips for Getting Started

Writing Your Story

Use this as another brainstorming page. Has this workbook generated any ideas about writing a story of your own? Jot down a few random thoughts.

Extra Space

More Memories

Write any further stories or memories here.

About the Author

Andrea Bargsley Vincent grew up in a fairly small suburb of Dallas, in Texas, where her imagination grew wild amid the wall-to-wall books of her mother's library.

Mrs. Vincent divides her time between studying gerontology and creating ways to help children become more comfortable and compassionate about the elderly. Her ultimate goal is to create positive relationships between the world's youth and senior citizens, either collectively through intergenerational programs or in separate capacities. She believes this relationship to be fundamental in the world for facing its largest elderly population ever.

Mrs. Vincent currently works for FirstLight Home Care in Northern Virginia. FirstLight hopes to make an impact on the lives of our elderly population by showing them kindness, compassion, and gratitude with every interaction.

Author of <u>Bite-Size Pieces of My Past</u>, Andrea Bargsley Vincent, currently studies gerontology and hopes to ultimately help the elderly live healthier, happier lives in the comfort of their own homes for as long as possible.

Use this simple, large print, fill-in-the-blank workbook while visiting loved ones, friends, neighbors, and residents of senior living communities.

It is an icebreaker for new caregivers.

It is an intimate conversation starter for loved ones.

It is a fun interaction tool for visitors.

It is a keepsake for future generations.

Trafford Publishing   ISBN 141201680-0
2333 Government Street, Suite 6E
Victoria, B.C. V8T 4P4, CANADA
Phone 250-383-6864   Toll-free 1-888-232-4444
Fax   250-383-6804   E-mail sales@trafford.com

Printed in the United States
By Bookmasters